To Anne, Allyn, and Farai, with gratitude and hugs
—A. L.

This book is a testament to the love and support of my husband, Ayo; my son, Sunday;
and my entire family. Your unwavering belief fuels my journey, and I am grateful for you all.
—F. S.

BEACH LANE BOOKS
An imprint of Simon & Schuster Children's Publishing Division
1230 Avenue of the Americas, New York, New York 10020
Text © 2024 by Aura Lewis and Farai Simoyi
Illustration © 2024 by Aura Lewis
BEACH LANE BOOKS and colophon are trademarks of Simon & Schuster, LLC.
Simon & Schuster: Celebrating 100 Years of Publishing in 2024
For information about special discounts for bulk purchases, please contact Simon & Schuster Special Sales at
1-866-506-1949 or business@simonandschuster.com.
The Simon & Schuster Speakers Bureau can bring authors to your live event. For more information or to book an event,
contact the Simon & Schuster Speakers Bureau at 1-866-248-3049 or visit our website at www.simonspeakers.com.
Book design by Sonia Chaghatzbanian
The text for this book was set in Cochin.
The illustrations for this book were rendered in mixed media.
Manufactured in China
0424 SCP
First Edition
2 4 6 8 10 9 7 5 3 1
Library of Congress Cataloging-in-Publication Data
Names: Lewis, Aura, author. | Simoyi, Farai, author..
Title: Dazzling Zelda : the story of fashion designer Zelda Wynn Valdes / by Aura Lewis ;
created in collaboration with Farai Simoyi.
Description: First edition. | New York ; London : Beach Lane Books, 2024. |
Includes bibliographical references. | Audience: Ages 4-8 | Audience: Grades 2-3 | Summary:
"The dazzling true story of Black fashion icon and design pioneer Zelda Wynn Valdes, whose dresses, gowns,
and costumes helped make people shine"— Provided by publisher.
Identifiers: LCCN 2023036382 (print) | LCCN 2023036383 (ebook) | ISBN 9781665918299 (hardcover) |
ISBN 9781665918305 (ebook)
Subjects: LCSH: Wynn, Zelda. | Fashion designers—United States—Biography—
Juvenile literature. | African American women costume designers—
Biography—Juvenile literature. | LCGFT: Biographies.
Classification: LCC TT505.W96 L49 2023 (print) | LCC TT505.W96 (ebook) |
DDC 746.9/2092 [B]—dc23/eng/20231201
LC record available at https://lccn.loc.gov/2023036382
LC ebook record available at https://lccn.loc.gov/2023036383

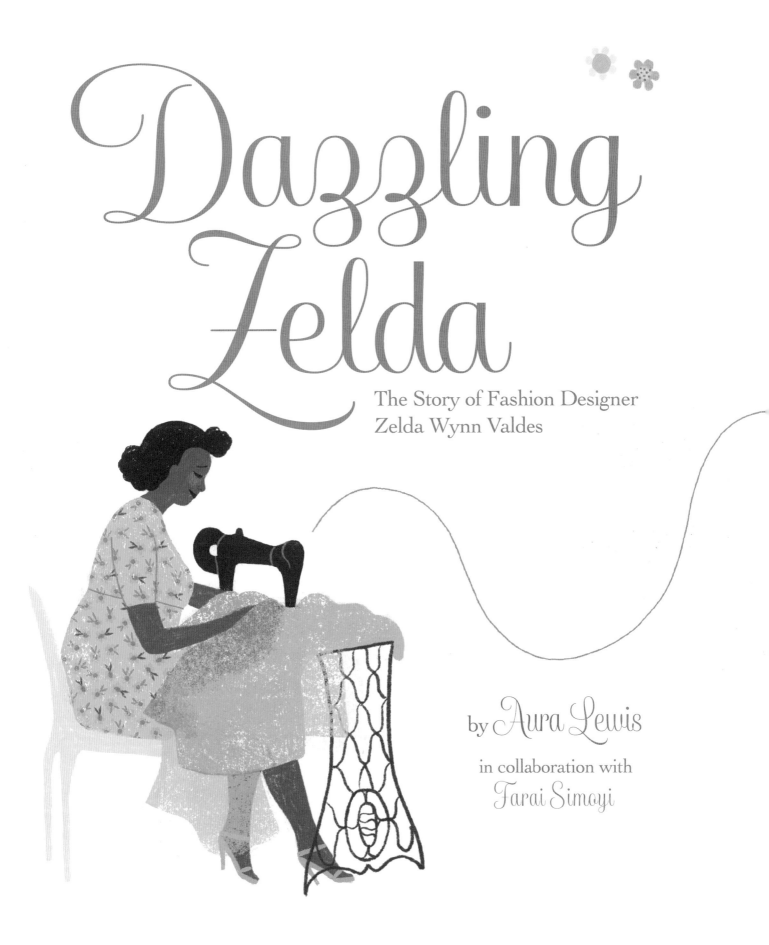

Dazzling Zelda

The Story of Fashion Designer
Zelda Wynn Valdes

by Aura Lewis

in collaboration with
Farai Simoyi

Beach Lane Books • New York   London   Toronto   Sydney   New Delhi

Zelda's home was always abuzz
with bright piano music,
clanging pots,
and sparkly laughs.

But her favorite sound was the soothing hum
of the sewing machine
in her grandmother's room.

Snip, snap, sew!

When Zelda announced she was making a dress,
her grandmother was skeptical.

"Daughter, you can't sew for me.
I'm too tall and too big."

But Zelda knew she could do it.

When she presented her grandmother
with a sensational dress, her family was dazzled.

Zelda was in love~

in love with sewing and sequins,
style and fashion!

She dreamed of designing dresses
to make people even more beautiful.

When Zelda was old enough,
she went to work in her uncle's shop.

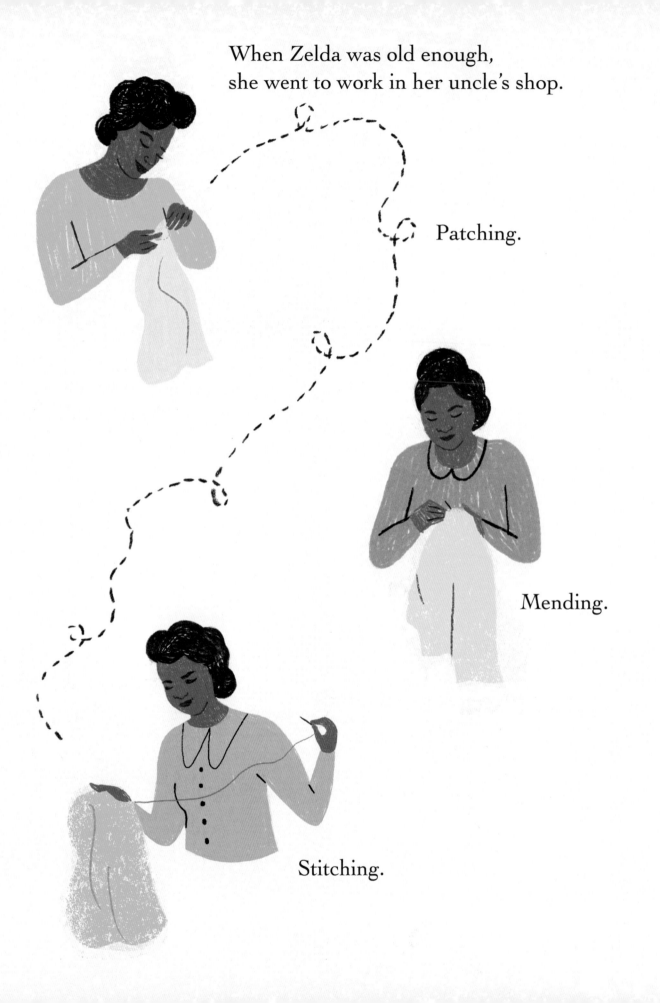

Patching.

Mending.

Stitching.

And making dresses when she could.

Soon Zelda was so busy,
she opened her very own boutique
in New York City,
the city of fashion and pizzazz.

Women of all colors, shapes, and sizes
came to her store.

Zelda dressed them for every occasion.

Simple-everyday dresses.

Elegant-evening dresses.

Snazzy-sporty dresses.

And her favorite:
glitzy-glittery-glamorous dresses.

The women loved Zelda's designs.
And Zelda loved making her garments fit just right.

But things were not always easy.

It was difficult for women like Zelda to make a name
for themselves in fashion during this time of segregation,
when laws and society attempted
to keep Black people and white people separate.

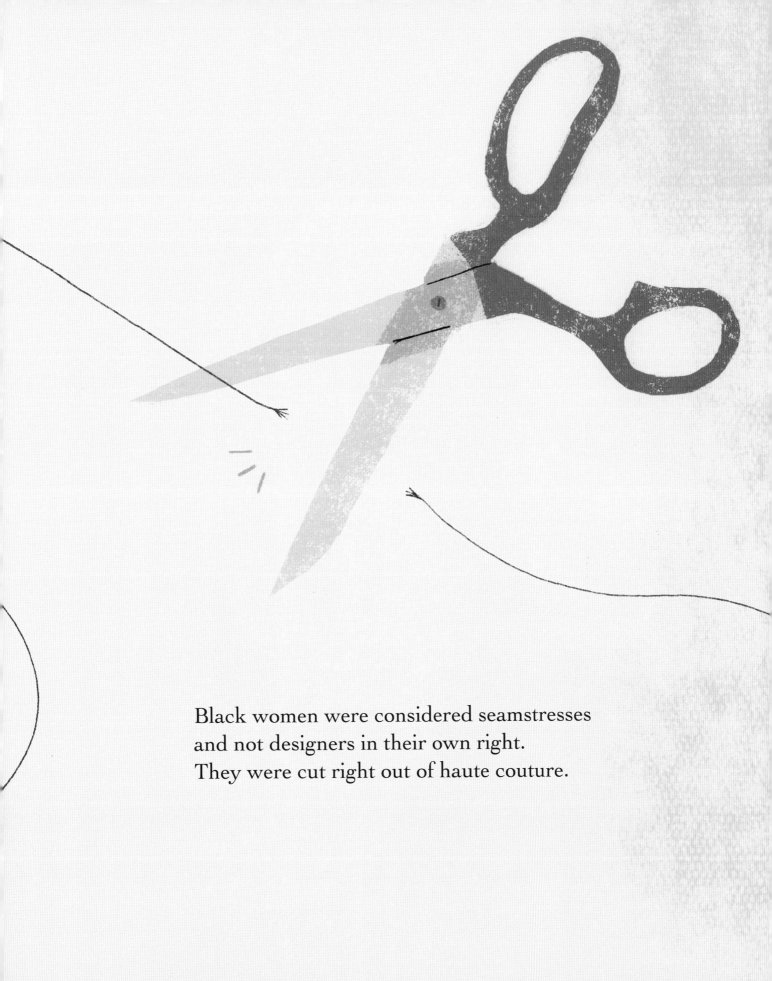

Black women were considered seamstresses
and not designers in their own right.
They were cut right out of haute couture.

Zelda worked harder and longer, day and night,
to make her designs even more exquisite
and to make her shop stand out.

And though the world outside was often harsh,
and though Zelda felt like she didn't quite fit in,
she did not give up.

Deep inside,
she knew she could do it.

Zelda wowed the crowds with her gowns.
The magazines were all abuzz.

"Elegant & Stunning"

"Extremely Fashionable"

"Show Stopping!"

Soon famous women
and glamorous stars
came to Zelda for their dresses.

Aretha Franklin

Marlene Dietrich

Josephine Baker

Zelda even made gowns for
Ella Fitzgerald, the Queen of Jazz.

There was only one little snag:
Ella sang all over the globe
and couldn't come in to be fitted in person.
So Zelda used her imagination
to make all of Ella's gowns!

Besides making dresses,
Zelda designed costumes too—
for shows on Broadway
and for the Dance Theatre of Harlem.

While her gowns were shaped like sculptures,
her costumes were light-as-air
so the dancers could twirl and flow.

Back then, all ballerinas had to wear pink tights,
no matter who they were
or what color their skin was.
This did not look right to Zelda.
She knew that dancers came in every shade
and that costumes should embrace their color.

So she rolled up her sleeves.
She knew just what to do!

Zelda colored the tights to match each dancer's skin.

Soon multihued pointe shoes and tutus
graced dancers' bodies everywhere.
Zelda's tights paved the way for the world of dance
to celebrate all shades of skin
and bring a rainbow to the stage.

Zelda did not stop there.
She worked day and night
to mentor young designers
and teach sewing and fashion
to those who couldn't go to school.

She wanted to help other Black artists
make their mark on the world,

just as she had become
a fashion designer,
a couturier,
a star.

Above all else,
Zelda dreamed of making
people beautiful.
She did just that,
and a great deal more—

she helped

make people shine!

More about Zelda

Zelda Wynn Valdes was an African American clothing designer who was born in Pennsylvania in the early 1900s and grew up in North Carolina. As a child, she trained as a classical pianist and learned how to sew dresses. When she was older, Zelda got a job stocking shelves in a clothing store and discovered a passion for fashion. In 1935, she worked for her uncle's dressmaking business in White Plains, New York, but yearned to make her own clothes. In 1948, Zelda opened a design studio and boutique, Zelda Wynn, which became the first Black-owned business on Broadway in New York City. Zelda worked hard to get her designs noticed by celebrities and influential people in the fashion world. Soon she began selling her dresses to singers like Ella Fitzgerald and Gladys Knight, actresses like Mae West, and performing artists like Josephine Baker. She even designed the bridal dress for the wedding of Maria Cole and jazz artist Nat King Cole.

In the 1950s, with her business doing extremely well, she opened Chez Zelda in the heart of Midtown Manhattan. By then she was a coveted designer for women all over the country, and her gowns cost nearly $1,000 each, which is about $12,000 today!

By the next decade, Zelda also became the director of a youth fashion and design workshop in Harlem, where she taught costume design. Additionally, Zelda was involved in the National Association of Fashion and Accessory Designers, which promoted Black designers in the fashion industry. Zelda was passionate about supporting young talent and the future of fashion.

In 1970, Zelda was invited to design special costumes for the Dance Theatre of Harlem. Over the next thirty years, Zelda designed for eighty-two different dance productions and influenced many trends in the costume design community. Zelda is credited as the first costume designer to match each dancer's tights and shoes to their skin tone through a special dyeing process. Her thoughtful design innovations shaped the future of inclusive costuming.

Even after Zelda shut down her business in 1989, she remained a passionate advocate for young designers and for the promotion of diversity in the fashion industry. Her dedication to change within the industry continued until she died in 2001.

Before Zelda's arrival on the fashion scene, most of the opportunities available to Black women were only as tailors or seamstresses. Zelda paved the way for Black women to take on lead roles in the world of design. Following Zelda's rise to fashion fame, other Black designers made significant strides of their own. Ruby Bailey was known for her flamboyant and Afrocentric designs, which were beloved by Harlem

artists and socialites. She worked as a master beader and was a peer of Zelda's at the National Association of Fashion and Accessory Designers. Ann Lowe is known today for designing First Lady Jacqueline Bouvier Kennedy's bridal gown in 1953, but at the time she was not credited as the designer by the fashion industry or by Jacqueline Kennedy because of her race. It was not until the mid-1960s that Lowe received recognition for her famous design. Once Ann Lowe gained recognition, she embarked on a journey of designing for the crème de la crème of American society, earning herself the title of "society's best kept secret."

Black women designers are still making big strides in the fashion industry. Tracy Reese gained global recognition when she created a custom dress for First Lady Michelle Obama in 2012. Anifa Mvuemba has worked with fashion icons like Beyoncé, Zendaya, and Sarah Jessica Parker. Kianga "Kiki Kitty" Milele has designed for musicians such as Nicki Minaj and Rihanna. In the 1990s, during the peak of hip-hop music and culture, April Walker became the first woman of color to establish multibillion-dollar streetwear brands that are still sold today. Aurora James's and Dumebi Iyamah's designs have been featured in major publications like *Vogue*, *Forbes*, *InStyle*, and *HuffPost*. These Black women designers have made a huge cultural impact in the world of Black fashion and continue to utilize their platforms to create opportunities for upcoming Black designers.

Sources

Christie, Shelby Ivey. "This Organization Made History for Black Talent in the Fashion Industry." *ZORA*, September 6, 2019. https://zora.medium.com/this-organization-made-history-for-black-talent-in-the-fashion-industry-ec15f49c5ad9.

Deihl, Nancy, editor. *The Hidden History of American Fashion: Rediscovering 20th-century Women Designers*. London: Bloomsbury, 2018.

Ford, Tanisha C. "Zelda Wynn Valdes: A Fashion Designer Who Outfitted the Glittery Stars of Screen and Stage." *New York Times*, January 2019. https://www.nytimes.com/interactive/2019/obituaries/zelda-wynn-valdes-overlooked.html.

Gabbara, Princess. "How Zelda Wynn Valdes Redefined Fashion." Shondaland, April 25, 2018. https://www.shondaland.com/live/style/a19992024/zelda-wynn-valdes/.

"Harlem's Ruby Bailey, a Legendary Fashion Pioneer in Harlem, NY (1912–2003)." *Harlem World Magazine*, March 4, 2022. https://www.harlemworldmagazine.com/harlems-ruby-bailey-fashion-pioneer-ny-1912-2003/.

Momodu, Samuel. "Zelda Barbour Wynn Valdes (1901–2001)." *BlackPast*, June 9, 2017. https://www.blackpast.org/african-american-history/valdes-zelda-barbour-wynn-1901-2001/.

There are conflicting birth years for Zelda; some sources say 1901, while others say 1905.

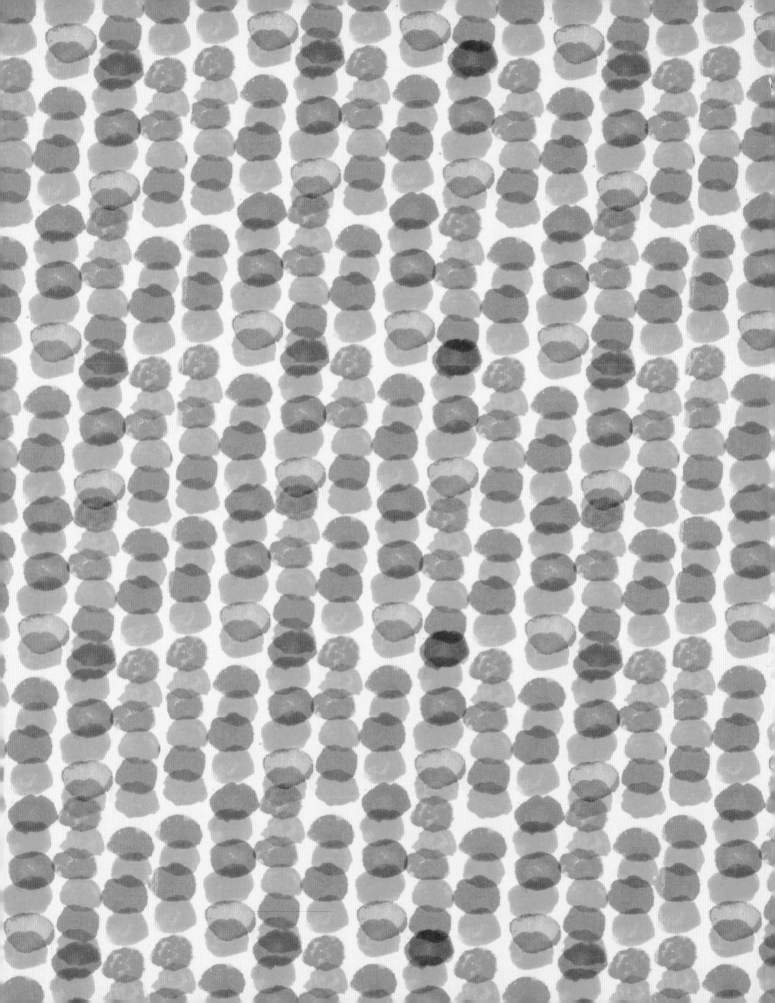